THE SIXTY 60 MINUTE MARRIAGE BUILDER

B U I L D E R

ROB PARSONS

THE SIXTY MINUTE MARRIAGE BUILDER

An Hour of Reading for a Lifetime of Love

BROADMAN
& HOLMAN
PUBLISHERS

Nashville, Tennessee

The Sixty-Minute Marriage Builder
© 1998, 2001 by Rob Parsons

ISBN-10: 0-8054-2562-4
ISBN-13: 978-0-8054-2562-8

Unless otherwise noted, Scripture quotations are from the Holy
Bible, New International Version, copyright © 1973, 1978, 1984
by International Bible Society.

Published by
Broadman & Holman Publishers, Nashville, Tennessee
Previously published under different cover and same title as
ISBN 0-8054-0178-4 (now OP)

Dewey Decimal Classification: 646.7
Subject Heading: MARRIAGE–UNITED STATES /
MARRIED PEOPLE–UNITED STATES–PSYCHOLOGY

Library of Congress Cataloging-in-Publication Data

Parsons, Rob, 1948–.
    The sixty minute marriage builder, Rob Parsons.
        p.   cm.
    ISBN 0-8054-0178-4 (pbk.)
    ISBN 0-8054-2562-4 (pbk.)
    1. Marriage–United States.   2. Married People–United
States–Psychology.
HQ536.P376   1998
646.7'8–dc21   97–42260
                                                          CIP

4 5 6 7 8 9 10   10 09 09 07 06 05

To Emily, age five.

Contents

Acknowledgments

As ever, I am indebted to lots of people. Thanks to Jonathan Booth, Lyndon Bowring, Charlie Colchester, Tom Beardshaw, Jim Boston, Jacqui Butler, Lisa Curtis, Susan Davies, Kate Hancock, Janie Lawry, Peter Mortimer, Helen Payton, Sheron Rice, Keith Tondeur, Steve Williams, and Janis Whipple, my editor.

And especially to Dianne, Katie, and Lloyd–thank you.

The Girl at the Zoo

The zoo had opened at nine and my son and I were its first customers. It was 2:30 in the afternoon when I saw the man. He wouldn't have caught my eye any earlier in the day but frankly I was tired of trying to tempt the seals out of the water, the gorillas out of their backstage dwellings, and had long since given up trying to wake a particularly nasty looking snake. I was in the terminal stages of what one parent called "zoo fatigue" and had bought an ice cream, found a seat, and turned my attention to watching humans.

As I sat I discovered I was watching a surefire nomination for the perfect father award. While other parents dozed on the grass, or just stared vacantly into the monkeys' cage, he gave his daughter his full attention. One moment he was lifting her to the elephants, the next kneeling beside her as he explained exactly why monkeys have red bottoms. (I wish I'd been close enough to hear his answer.) It wasn't just her mind he fed; in the space of thirty minutes this child had consumed a bag of potato chips, a lollipop in the shape of a bear, and a bag of popcorn.

Finally, even he got tired, left his daughter tormenting an iguana, and slumped onto the seat next to me. By now the man was my hero and I told him so. I'm not sure what I expected; perhaps a shrug of the shoulders and, "Any father would do it." That didn't happen. What I got was a conversation that lasted almost an hour.

His marriage had broken up two months earlier and his wife had custody of their only child. This was "his Saturday" with Emily. He pulled from his wallet a dog-eared photograph; in the forefront a woman sat in a hospital bed holding a newborn child. He was standing next to her with his arm on her shoulder. They were both gazing down at the baby.

If I had to find a word to caption that faded Polaroid I suppose I would choose *hope*. They had plans for that child. Her nursery had been ready a full four weeks before the birth, but the dreams stretched far beyond baby-hood. This was *their* child.

Suddenly the man became animated. He began to tell me about Emily's first words; about the date of the first faltering steps; and of the time when she was three and he and Claire had lost her for a moment in a department store crowded with Christmas shoppers.

It would have been a hard or foolish man who would have walked away from him that day, and as I listened I felt a tremendous surge of sorrow. But not just for him. I imagined Emily's mother waiting for her to come back. Somebody who would look behind the curtains and, hearing the bell, come quickly to the door, and mumbling a good-bye to the one who was now a stranger, would bring her in. That mother would do her very best for her child. But it would be harder than she ever imagined.

I also felt sorrow for the child who now sat swinging one leg over the edge of a bench and rather hopefully throwing peanuts to sparrows. She was a statistic—a child of a broken home. But whatever did that mean? What had been broken, how had it happened, and could it ever be mended?

And I wondered if anybody could have said anything, or written something that could have given these three a better chance. This little book is my response to that day.

The Sixty-Minute Marriage Builder is a short book. I have written it so you can read it in an hour. At regular intervals there are sixty-second pages that sum up what has gone before, and there is just one "one-second page"! Scattered throughout the book are "Action Points." I asked various people to share simple lessons they had learned in their marriages; choose those that may help you.

All kinds of people will read this book. Some will be at the beginning of their lives together, others going though some traumatic time that threatens to cause them to part. Some will have known the pain of divorce. I have talked about children but I know that not all will be parents. In that and other areas simply skip what isn't of interest to you.

You may have noticed that the book is dedicated to Emily, and yes, she is the child I met that day at the zoo. Every day, hundreds of children are affected by their parents' divorce. She represents each one of them. I have many hopes for this book. I want it to be a help to those considering marriage; I believe that it can make strong marriages more able to face the hard times that will surely come; but above all I wrote it "for the sake of the children." My dream is that because of this little book some other Emily will never lose her father.

Bring on the Clowns

When I was five years old my father took me and three friends to the circus. I really can't remember what impressed the others but I fell in love with the clowns. The reason for such high emotion in a small boy is not hard to figure out. Of course they juggled without dropping, fell without hurting, and had a total disregard for authority. For all those reasons they were heroes. But compelling as all those qualities were, it wasn't any one of them that so captivated me. No, I fell in love with the clowns because they were never sad.

I can't quite remember why that was so important to me at such a tender age. I suppose it's because in my sixty months or so on this planet I had known some trauma. There was the time the rabbit died; and the day the head came off my favorite soldier. Even now I can taste the salt of the tears those events brought. But the clowns always laughed; no sorrow touched them—they were immune.

I loved them for that reason until I was nine. Two days after my birthday, I watched a film on television about a circus. As I sat glued to my seat, the camera suddenly moved away from the ring to a nearby caravan. On the door was written in fancy lettering, "The home of Coco." By the wonders of technology I was taken inside the inner sanctuary of the greatest clown who had ever lived.

Yet my hero sat on a bed, tears running down his face; and by his side lay a mask that smiled up at him. I cried too.

Thousands of people feel condemned to wear the smile of the clown. They feel that nobody could understand the trauma they are going through. I often start one of our marriage seminars in the same way. I look out at an audience of perhaps a thousand people and say, "Nobody has told me about you. Nobody called me last night and said, 'By the way, Bob and Carol will be in the audience. They're going through a tough time—say something that might help them.'" And I say that because if I don't, people will think that somebody *has* been talking to me.

During the seminar I will speak of those in whose hearts love has died. They have been married for eleven years, they have three children, and they long to be free of their husband or wife. Sometimes they imagine getting the news that he or she has died, and they are ashamed; but they dream of the freedom, and wonder about the new person they will meet, who will be so very different.

I talk of those who are experiencing financial trauma that makes it hard to survive, let alone feel in love with each other, and those whose sexual relationship is all but dead. I talk of the man at the very start of an affair. He has come to the seminar with his wife, and she has no idea what is going on. Even as I speak he thinks of his new relationship.

They are in every audience. But so often they believe they are alone. Although the media screams at them that this is common—although they know friends going through similar circumstances—they still have this incredible sense of isolation. It whispers in their ear, "Nobody could understand, let alone change your situation." And so often it's that sense of isolation, the way we have so long worn the mask and said, "Oh, fine thanks" that eventually kills love; that makes it hard to find answers.

Removing the Mask

These are not easy issues. I know that better than most. I have spoken to over one hundred thousand people about marriage in cultures across the world. I receive thousands of letters, many of which would break your heart. I have no illusions about the difficulties that we experience in our married lives—not least because my wife, Dianne, and I have been married for over twenty-five years. We have known difficult times, and there may be some tough ones ahead—none of us are immune. I have counseled those who have been physically, sexually, and mentally abused; for some of those it has been necessary to leave their homes in order to protect themselves and their children. Nevertheless, I have observed that many marriages break up not because of large issues but because of everyday pressures that build until they are unbearable.

I have come to believe that marriages can be revolutionized by somebody speaking plainly about the traumas which hit many of us, and breaking through the sense of isolation that makes us feel, "this is only happening to us." When that happens it can have a dramatic effect. A woman wrote to me recently after one of our seminars and said, "Thank you for giving our children back their father."

At the start of *The Sixty-Minute Marriage Builder* slip the mask to the floor–you can always retrieve it if you need it. The way forward is honesty, and believing in your heart that what is happening to you is not unique. Others have been there, and some have found a love again that they thought had gone forever.

In this hour together we'll look at ten goals. If you have a good marriage these will make it stronger; if you are going through difficult times together they can revolutionize your relationship. Each of them is important, but in my opinion number one is in a class of its own. . . .

"A coward is incapable
of exhibiting love:
it is the prerogative
of the brave."
    –Mahatma Ghandi

To Develop
Effective Communication

We Don't Talk Anymore

It was a warm September afternoon. It had been a busy day in the law practice and she was my last client. She had refused to tell my secretary the nature of her problem, and as I offered her coffee I still had no idea. She looked composed and businesslike, but that may not have accounted for much. I have long since given up trying to learn much about clients by their appearance. (I was cured of that twenty years ago when on a Wednesday morning, a man I would have sworn was homeless dumped thirty-five thousand dollars in cash on my desk and told me to be sure to complete a purchase of some property by the following Monday.)

"How can I help you?" I said to the woman.

"I think my marriage is over."

"How long have you been married?"

"Seventeen years."

"Do you have children?"

"A thirteen-year-old boy and a ten-year-old girl."

"Why has your relationship broken down so badly?"

"He has made me an island."

11

"I'm sorry—would you repeat that?"

"He has made me into an island. He will not talk to me about anything. In the early years of our marriage we would spend hours talking together, but something has happened to him. It seems he can't talk to me. When he gets in I ask him about his day and I get the same grunt that I get from my teenager when I ask him about how things are going at school. But it's deeper than that. We've had problems before, but we could always talk about them. Have you any idea what it is like to share your home, your body, your life with somebody who will not communicate with you? Eventually you die inside."

She would have gone on but just then the coffee arrived; as I poured it my mind went to another client who had sat in the same chair just four hours earlier.

I knew Tom and his wife well, which made it harder for me to understand the man I saw in front of me earlier that day. I had never thought him a very emotional person. He had risen to the top of his profession; he was in every sense a "make-it-happen" kind of man. He always looked assured, in control, and some said a little daunting. Yet the second he walked into my office I could see he'd been crying. The note was crumpled and he handed it to me as if it had a life of its own. The tape was still on the back where he had pulled it from the refrigerator door.

> *I need time to think—I've taken the kids with me. Will be away for a couple of days. I'll be in touch soon.*
> *Love, Susan*

I listened as he poured out his heart to me. He couldn't understand what the problem was. He had always provided for his family. They had a fine house, took frequent vacations, and he genuinely loved his wife.

But the crumpled note wasn't the only piece of paper he had brought. In trying to find out where his wife was, he had gone through her drawer and found a half-finished letter she had written to a friend:

Tom and I were so in love when we got married. It was nothing for us in those early days to sit and talk for hours. Even when we weren't speaking, there was a sense that we knew what the other was feeling. It's hard to know when we really grew apart. Tom's job became more and more demanding and I had the children to see to. It may have been that I gave them too much attention and he felt excluded but, looking back, I honestly feel if I hadn't been speaking to them, I wouldn't have been talking to anybody.

He comes home so tired he can hardly say "hello," let alone tell me about his day or even pretend to be interested in mine. I hate it. I long to speak to him. Sometimes, after we had made love, I would for a moment believe he felt close to me and, as we lay there, I would begin to tell him so much of what I had been longing to say. But so often, as I shared my heart, I would realize that he was already asleep. And then a strange thing happened. I learned to live without him. Oh, I washed his clothes and cooked and tried hard to be a wife to him, but inside I learned to live apart from him. It was as if something inside me said, "you're on you're own—for your sake and the kids' sake, face it and learn to live with it."

**"It is not only
necessary to love,
it is necessary
to say so."**

— French saying

A Creeping Separateness

Several times during my legal career I have been present at postmortems. I can remember on one occasion being in the mortuary for many hours as two pathologists tried to ascertain the exact cause of death. My client had been arrested but had claimed that his relative had died of natural causes. For over an hour these experts poured over the body and then, just as it seemed they would never find anything conclusive, one of them took a magnifying glass, leaned in close and exclaimed, "I think we have it–yes–look just here." My client was charged with murder.

I have come to believe that when love dies, so often the real cause of death is not the most obvious one. Not every marriage that I have seen break up has had incredible conflict, not every one has known sexual difficulties or an affair. No, the real killer is often hidden–they have simply stopped talking to each other.

Lack of communication doesn't mean not talking about anything. It means not talking about anything that matters. There comes a point in many marriages where one of the partners either cannot or will not discuss issues that are vital to the other.

One husband described the process of a relationship in which communication has died as "a creeping separateness." Such people can be great communicators in other settings. She has several friends with whom she shares the most intimate details of her life, and he at work may be the very life and soul of the party, but they have little to say to each other now.

There is not a marriage in the world that has not gone through some of this. When we have gone through difficult times in our relationship Dianne has said, "How come you can spend an hour on the phone to somebody from work and yet find it hard to talk to me for five minutes?"

All kinds of reasons have been suggested as to why we find it so hard to communicate. It's no secret that men in particular find it difficult. Some have said that men have a built-in incapacity to share their hearts in depth. There may be some truth in that. But watch a man at the beginning of an affair. He sits with his secretary in his car and talks a mile a minute. She says, "My husband would never talk to me like this." He replies, "My wife would never listen as you do." What is happening? His wife used to complain that he'd had a conversation bypass operation. Has it suddenly been reversed? No, it's simply that this couple at the beginning of their affair are not taking each other for granted. Even for them that day will come fast—but just now the sheer excitement keeps the conversation flowing.

It's so very easy to take each other for granted in a marriage. I often meet men and women who once found it so hard to make time to talk, yet who would now give anything for the chance to do just that. I have a friend whose marriage went through a difficult period some years ago. He is a typical overbusy executive who thrills at the sound of a telephone ringing and has spent much of his life saying to both his wife and children, "Later—next weekend—we'll make time then." But he changed. He saw that although he was highly successful, he was about to lose everything that really mattered to him. For the past eight years he has "dated" his wife every Tuesday night. Sometimes it's a meal out, often nothing that grand, but they have learned to talk again, and to give each other the dignity of knowing that they matter.

Of course what many people crave is not somebody to talk to them but somebody who will actually listen. One of the greatest compliments you can pay another person is to listen with your eyes. When we do that we say in effect, "I'm with you." It gives people dignity; it's why we should always bend to talk to toddlers.

And what of those two people who walked into my office on the same day in September? The woman phoned the next day to ask us to put things on hold. But what of the man with the crumpled note? He did a strange thing. He wrote his wife a letter. Sometimes you can say things in writing that would be harder face-to-face. Here's a little of what he wrote:

> I had no idea what my refusal to talk with you was doing to our relationship. Life has been so busy and I suppose I always assumed there would be tomorrow. But for me now that

tomorrow is impossible. I can only imagine how isolated you must have felt and I know you have no reason to believe that I can change. But I have lost you all and I want you back.

Two years later, I got a letter from his wife. She said, "I'd be a fool to say that everything was wonder-ful—there is so much we have to work through. But now we talk things through. When we feel hurt we say so, and we've learned to *make time* to talk. He has changed so much. I don't know what you said to him that day in your office, but it worked."

The truth is, I didn't say a thing.

ACTION PAGE

~ Try to have an evening once a week for just the two of you. Defend it with your life.

~ Listen with your eyes.

~ Take walks together more often.

~ Don't confuse your partner's need for space with rejection.

∞

"An archaeologist is the
best husband any woman
can have:
the older she gets,
the more interested
he is in her."

— *Agatha Christie*

To Make Time

Near our home is an exercise club. It is quite fascinating. Before you ask what particular exercises have caught my attention, I must tell you that to date none have, but I have found the building a wonderful place to "people watch." They come in all shapes and sizes and in all manner of clothing. Young men with tiny waists come in their spandex and middle aged men without tiny waists come in track suits they have not used since they were in high school.

But the truly remarkable thing is where these people park their cars. They do so in ever increasing numbers in the spaces marked for disabled people just outside the entrance. The club has tried all manner of things to stop them from being so selfish but they will not comply. Isn't this strange? They rush to their club after work and put their bodies through all manner of torture in an effort to get fit, but they will not walk an extra twenty yards from their cars and so they choose the disabled spaces. If you were brave enough to interrupt them in the middle of an aerobic nightmare and ask them why they do this, they would say, "I was in a hurry."

We are a society in a hurry. Someone has convinced us that fast is good. The other day I saw an ad for a car costing over forty thousand dollars. It was headed, "Secs Appeal" and it declared that this

22

particular car could go from zero to sixty miles per hour 2.7 seconds faster than its nearest rival. Isn't that good news? We roar off in this modern wonder and get to the end of the road way ahead of the poor creature in the Ferrari behind us. We turn to gloat . . . and the 2.7 seconds is gone.

Our ancestors submitted to time; we do battle with it. They painted portraits; if we can't get our vacation photos back in an hour we feel put out. One of the curators at the National Zoo in Washington D. C. said recently that most visitors think hippopotamuses stay under the water for long periods of time. Actually, he said, the average is ninety seconds, but "the tourists haven't got the patience to wait."

One Thousand, Four Hundred and Forty Minutes

Such time pressure is also killing relationships. A recent National Opinion Poll[1] survey showed that the average father spends less than five minutes a day in one-to-one communication with his children; those same children watched an average of three hours of television a day. But it's hard to build relationships without time. Those men may be very successful at work, but many will discover that when they do have time for their families, the children have other ideas. The door of childhood will have closed. One father put it like this, "When they are small they are suckers for the 'we'll do it later' routine. Actually it's not them we're fooling but us. 'One of those days' turns out to be 'none of those days.'"

It can happen in a marriage. There are marriages of twenty years and in all that time they have not spent twenty minutes sitting in a quiet room and actually listening to each other. Not twenty minutes in twenty years; but it is impossible to keep love alive without time. I have no doubt that the husband of the woman who wrote the following letter gave her everything except his time. And yet when he loses her he will be genuinely surprised and say, as I used to so often, "But I'm doing all this for you and the children."

> John and I were deeply in love when we got married. We struggled during the first few years especially with financial problems, but then he got a promotion; that required him to work longer hours. He comes home late every evening. I have so much to tell him but he doesn't feel like talking. I make his meal and he eats it alone. Believe me, there are times when we go for a month or two without having a real conversation. There is no closeness or warmth between us, yet he wants to have sex with me at the end of the day. There we are lying in bed having had no communication between us in weeks and he expects me to be passionate and responsive. I tell you, I cannot do it. Sure I go along with it but I get nothing out

of it. And when the two minute trip is over and John is asleep I lie there resenting him. I feel like a prostitute. Can you believe that? I feel used for having sex with my own husband. My self-esteem is rock bottom. I'm a lousy mother and a terrible wife.[2]

That man's overbusy lifestyle was killing his marriage. Having said that, the woman in the next piece of correspondence makes him look laid back.

After the baby was born I went straight back to work—and I mean straight back. It seemed that one minute I was pushing the baby out, and the next moment on the telephone to a client. Why should I complain—I've got help in the house, I've got every time-saving gadget that humans have ever devised. I've got a great career. The only thing I haven't got is time. I haven't got time for my husband, my child, and I haven't got time for me. People think I'm the typical "make-it-happen" woman. The truth is, my life is falling apart.

Some years ago somebody talked to me about trying to manage the mound of paper that comes into our lives every day. She gave me a piece of advice with regard to the mail at home: "Always open it over a trash can. You will find you can rip up 90% of it immediately and you'll know you've really got it under control when you rip it all up without opening any of it!" I try to remember what she said. But the other day a piece of junk mail addressed to me personally got through the system.

> *Dear Underachiever,*
> *I'm not trying to insult you or demean you (I think,* Thank goodness he's not trying!*) I just happen to believe that most people are underachievers. These unfulfilled men and women never reach potential. I believe in being a "no-limit person" and I can make you one.*

It was 7:00 A.M. as I stood bleary-eyed, letter in hand, in the hallway of my home, gazing down at my slippers and wondering, "Would I like to be a 'no-limit' person?" Would I like to be able to run a full-time job, sit on endless committees, learn crochet and Italian in my spare time and still build a strong relationship with my wife and children? Would I like to say "Yes" every time somebody asks me to do something and still have space for my own family? Do I wish that I was Superman and could fly and juggle at the same time? You bet I do. *But I can't.*

And the reason I can't do it all is that time is limited. Whether I am rich or poor, clever or dull, I have exactly the same amount of time as everybody else. But it is limited. Each day comes to me full of one thousand four hundred and forty minutes. By the time I wake, realize that it's not Saturday but Monday, and get dressed, I have just one thousand left. And every day I spend all of them; and every choice I make as to how I will spend them precludes another option.

There is no shortage of timesaving devices, fast food, and day planners that allow us to schedule every minute of the day. The only thing we don't have any more of is time. But none of us would live like this if we thought that life would always be this busy and we would never have time to build good relationships with our husband, wife, or children. And so we fool ourselves that this is a busy *period* of our lives and that when it is over we will have more time. We wait patiently for that quieter day, but for most of us it's an illusion—the day never comes.

I have made many mistakes in this area, but one day it dawned on me that although I was relatively successful, my family was slipping through my fingers. I told that story in my last book, *The Sixty-Minute Father.* Wherever in the world that book is sold, people thank me for one line in particular. It urges us that while we are busy building careers not to forget to invest time in building relationships with those we love. If we don't give time there, we may be successful outside the home, but will look back with tremendous regret.

And the line. Oh, it's very simple:

Nobody ever said on their deathbed, "I wish I'd spent more time at the office."

SIXTY-SECOND PAGE

"So often it's the sense of isolation, the way we have so long worn the mask and said, 'Oh, fine thanks' that eventually kills love."

"The real killer is often hidden . . . they have simply stopped talking to each other."

"How come you can spend an hour on the phone to someone from work and yet find it hard to talk to me for five minutes?"

"What many people crave is not somebody to talk to them but somebody who will actually listen."

"I believe there are marriages of twenty years plus and in all that time they have not spent twenty minutes sitting in a quiet room and actually listening to each other."

"Although I was relatively successful, my own family was slipping through my fingers."

"A woman marries a man
with the ridiculous notion
that she can change him
and he with the foolish
idea that she will be
the same forever."

To Survive Conflict

Paul and Caroline had been married for six years and they always used to boast they'd never had an argument. Friends didn't believe it, but it was true. That is, it *was* true until Christmas Eve last year. Neither of them can remember exactly how it started except that it had something to do with Christmas tree lights and a roll of tape. But if this couple had not argued for six years, they made up for it in that remarkable hour between six and seven o'clock on that evening of goodwill. As the fight intensified, hurts came tumbling out that had lay hidden for years, the oldest being something that occurred on the afternoon of their wedding. They didn't say a word to each other for three days, and she honestly thought their marriage could end. By New Year's Day they had begun to grunt at each other and now they're fine except that they argue every two months. They've decided it's much healthier.

Was it a good thing that this couple had never had a fight? No. Their problem was they didn't argue enough. Few people enjoy conflict but in itself it's not a bad thing. The important consideration is how we deal with it. Having said this, there are some ways of handling conflict that are surefire guarantees that the warfare will escalate and perhaps end up causing permanent injury. Here are four classic "bad moves."

Bad move #1:
Forget the issue—attack the person

Imagine that Sue has forgotten her son's dental appointment—again. Her husband Dave spots the appointment card lying under the pile of junk mail in the kitchen and says, "You forgot again, didn't you?" Now had he left it there, they could have had an argument about why she forgot, but he decides to abandon the issue and attack her *person*. "You are such a useless wife and mother." It wasn't the first time he had said it but the second it was out of his mouth he knew what he had done; still, even he didn't know the long-term effect. She never forgot those words and the way he made her feel that day.

The principle works the same with children. Your daughter will recover from a bit of conflict over a poor school report but she may not recover if you decide to attack her person—"You are so stupid. Why can't you be more like your sister? You are going to be a loser forever."

Bad move #2:
Widen the issue

With this one, instead of just arguing over the situation in hand we try to think of other unrelated events to give us a bit more firepower. It goes something like this, "How come you forgot the appointment again? You are such a useless wife and mother," and then, *"that's why last year's holiday with my mother was such a disaster."* Now the fascinating thing is the person who has this tactic used against her does not normally say, "What on earth has last year's holiday with your mother got to do with a dental appointment?" No, she widens the argument as well. "Yes I'm useless. And you're so great you've been passed over for a promotion four times." The fuse is now lit. Stand well back.

Bad move #3: Bring out the old mortar bombs

Every marriage has at least six of these hidden away. We bring them out when our back is against the wall and we need some heavy weaponry. They could involve sex, the "Honey do" list, weight, the way we discipline or don't discipline the children. Typical classics will draw on past events with in-laws, holidays, and money. Sometimes we feel ashamed of using them because they are so old, so we preface them with, "You'll never change," or "You always . . . ," or "You never . . ." Other phrases that freshen them up a little are, "I can never forget when . . ." or "The problem with you is that you are still . . ."

The real disadvantage in using them is they don't allow for change, or that somebody may be sorry about the past. Worse still, they show a lack of innovation in the art of arguing. Lay them down.

If only to find new ones.

Bad move #4:
Never lose an argument

There is nothing more certain to create terminal conflict in a marriage than one of the partners being brilliant with words. These creatures always have the final say. They have the ability to twist, manipulate, quote expert authority, and generally make you wish you hadn't bothered to start this particular fight. And they really believe they win arguments. What they don't see is what they leave behind—the unresolved anger, the bitterness inside, and a growing resentment of not being able to put your position forward. There is only one hope for such people. They must learn to lose arguments—to understand that winning is normally not nearly as important as it appears to be—to back off a little and give the other person space to say what he or she feels. When we learn to do this, we discover two things. First: conflict gets resolved faster. Second: the day after, we can't even remember what the argument was about.

Any of these "four bad moves" can turn a harmless argument into World War III, but even if we deal with conflict well, there are some situations where the only solution lies a little deeper than technique. . . .

Memories

It is said that time gives events a rosier hue. I believe it must be true.

Once in a while I come across people I was in school with. They hated the lessons, the teachers, and me. Now in some far corner of a department store we meet and shake each other's hand as if we had just discovered David Livingstone in the Men's Department. We set our shopping down, and amble down the years together. It almost always ends in the same way. We both vow to meet on a regular basis, contact the rest of the class of 1967, including Donald Griffiths who is now apparently operating a night-club in Abu Dhabi, and have a reunion at least once a year until we all die.

It's not just school days. Time has a trick or two with regard to parenting. What is it that allows us to look back on previous years of our children's lives with hardly a hint of a scream? At the time we were often gibbering wrecks, but now we hear ourselves talk with affection about the time that little Nick, (now 32–then two-and-a-half) tipped a whole can of gloss paint over the new carpet. It's because memory so often searches for the best.

But here is a mystery. If time is so clever at flushing from our minds the mini-horrors of the past, then why do we find it so hard to forget those occasions when somebody we love has hurt us badly. It could be the memory of the affair or the way we were treated when we needed support so badly. One man said, "You don't realize what a good memory you've got until you try with all your heart to forget something." Time and again people say to me, "I simply can't forget–I wish I could." Perhaps we can't erase those memories—only as an act of the will, decide not to nurse them. But we can forgive.

When Anne told Jack about the affair it was already over. She wasn't sure what she had expected him to do, and in her mind she had run over dozens of possibilities, including his leaving. What she didn't expect was nothing. No comment, no tears, no rage, just silence—for almost two months. Finally she wrote him a letter:

> Jack, if I could rewind this last year, I would do so at any cost. I just don't know what made me do what I did. I know we were going through a bad time, but nothing that justified my doing this to you. I love you and I love our children, but if we are to have any chance of staying together I need to ask you something that I don't deserve. I need you to forgive me. I don't need you to tell me again how wrong I've been. I know that now. I just need you to forgive me.

The road back for them began with that letter and with his sobbing like a child for a whole day. But he did forgive her. Together they decided that day to begin again, to do all they could to forget the past. It's not an easy path; he still sometimes wakes with that old feeling in the pit of his stomach, but as an act of the will he has vowed to let go of his hurt. It happened seven years ago and to this day he has never thrown it at her, never raised it when losing an argument over something else, and they have found love again—in spite of it all.

Forgiveness is not deciding to become a doormat. A man who cannot decide between his mistress and his wife and comes home weekends, goes again on a Monday, and who says like a five-year-old, "I want both of you," does not need forgiveness as much as he needs something that will clarify his mind. Sometimes this will be a wife saying, "I love you more than you know but I cannot go on sharing you like this. It's time for you to decide."

Forgiveness is not magical; we can ask too much of it. Sometimes we expect things to be as they were between us immediately, but that may take some time.

I remember at the end of a seminar a young couple waiting patiently to speak with me. They held back until they were sure the auditorium was empty and then he told me his story. He had an affair the year before. He said, "I told my wife what I did, and I asked for her forgiveness. I took my wedding ring off and said, 'Don't put that back on my finger until you can trust me again.' " And then he smiled, lifted his hand and said, "Last month she put it back on my finger."

He was relieved, but I turned to see how she was reacting. Her head was bowed. I said to him, "Forgive me if I'm wrong, but I think when she put that ring back on your finger she was not saying, 'I trust you again.' She was saying, 'With all my heart I *want* to trust you again.' "

She raised her head and said, "That's how I feel."

It will take time for this couple to build trust again, but they have begun. What would have festered and grown like a cancer in secret is dealt with. We need forgiveness like that, not just in the big issues, but in the small everyday hurts that affect every relationship.

Forgiveness feels pain but doesn't hoard it; it allows tomorrow to break free of yesterday. It is always hard, sometimes foolish, and at its heart, God-like.

There is no hope for us without it.

ACTION PAGE

~ Never go to sleep not talking. (It may be a long night!)

~ Never bring your partner down in public.

~ Be the first to say "sorry."

~ Criticize less. Discover the power of praise.

Husband to wife
as they arrive at a party:

"And don't try to stop me
each time I say,
'Stop me if
you've heard this.'"

To Accept What I Can't Change

I was twelve years old and puny when I first saw the advertisement and almost fourteen and still puny by the time I had saved enough to send off for the course. For twelve long days I waited for the postman to deliver the package that was going to change my life. It arrived on a Wednesday. It would have been unthinkable to have opened it in view of my family so I hurried upstairs to the bedroom. The contents were not quite as bulky as the box seemed to indicate but nevertheless they held the power of promise.

From the front cover of a glossy book a man beamed out at me; his name was Charles Atlas. He promised me that if I followed his secret, dynamic exercise program, not only would bullies stop kicking sand in my face, but it would be impossible to settle on a beach for five minutes without girls bothering me. I so desperately wanted to be bothered.

The thought of this small boy rising religiously at six, and putting his body through all manner of contortions fills me now with a desire to both laugh and cry. I was promised I would see a difference after just ten days. I did. On day nine, while finely honing an intricate muscle that dwelt deep in the recesses of my shoulder, I sprained my neck. I had to wear a collar all summer and walked for a month with a lopsided head. I lay on beaches, my head supported with several towels, an object of pity. Nobody kicked sand in my face, and no girls bothered me.

We smile at the efforts of a small boy to change himself; to try to become somebody he cannot really be. But we so often attempt the same with those we love.

It is without doubt one of the most poignant letters I have ever received:

> I was a disappointment to my father. He wanted a son. He never hugged me, praised me, or told me he loved me. I realize he was a product of his generation and I have forgiven him, but my self-esteem is very low, I am often depressed and I am riddled with guilt. *I am eighty-five years old.*

I have thought so much about this woman. I have imagined her as a child running home with drawings she had done for her father, as a teenager trying hard to be the kind of daughter that would make him proud, and even as a woman choosing the career that he would approve of. She had tried so hard to earn her father's love. But she could not succeed. The only way to please this man was to become somebody she could not be.

To live under such a pressure is utterly exhausting. Other people may have loved that young girl, and some may have praised her, but the one man she wanted to never did. And he followed her. She was pursued by her father through her childhood years, and then as a young adult. Even after his death it was as if his ghost was at her shoulder. He never left her and now she is near to death herself and still he waits for her to be the person she cannot be.

It can happen in marriage. I have known many people who look at other couples and wish that their partner were more like their friend's. They whisper, "If only Jim were more like Steve," or "You're so lucky having Vicky." Sometimes it is physical things that they want their partner to change. One of the saddest things I saw on television was a woman who was married to a plastic surgeon. In an effort to please her husband she had already had ten cosmetic operations on various parts of her body. She smiled confidently and said, "He'll never leave me. If he gets tired of me he can change the way I look."

Change can be a good thing. We all want our partners to change in some way. But the trouble comes when we want our partner to become somebody they cannot be. It would not be difficult to love if our partner was everything we wanted him or her to be, but if our relationship is to survive the long haul we have to learn to love a little differently; we have to learn to love not just "because of," but "in spite of."

There is a great difficulty here; it is that we live in a culture that has forgotten how to love like that.

Everything screams at us, "You deserve the best." The tragedy is we come to believe it.

We imagine the kind of person who would make us completely happy. If only he or she were thinner or fatter or wittier or stronger or better with the children. We may think we want a partner who is attractive, humorous, good with finances, a brilliant cook or fix-it specialist, and a sexual athlete. But the person you are married to cannot be all of those. And when we are consumed with the idea of the kind of person we want our spouse to be, we so often miss the person that he or she really is.

Sometimes after a marriage is over the partners will look back and wonder, "Why were those things such a big deal to me, when he was kind, and always there for me?"; "Why was her dress size so much more important to me than the person that she was?"

Perhaps we should consider something G. K. Chesterton said: "The way to love anything is to realize it might be lost."

SIXTY-SECOND PAGE

"Winning an argument is normally not nearly as important as it appears to be."

"You don't realize what a good memory you've got until you try with all your heart to forget something."

"Forgiveness feels pain but doesn't hoard it, it allows tomorrow to break free of yesterday."

"The trouble comes when we want our partner to be somebody he or she cannot be."

GOAL FIVE

To Be a Ghostbuster

Will you laugh just like your mother,
Will you sigh like your old man?
Will some things skip a generation
Like I've heard they often can?
Are you a poet or a dancer, a devil or a clown?
Or a strange new combination of things
we've handed down?[3]

—Marc Cohn

I first caught sight of her as I left the bus station. She was moving towards me, shuffling and muffled under an old coat tied with a piece of string. She had just foraged in one dumpster and was now moving towards the next. As she walked she pushed the grocery cart. No doubt many women had pushed it as she did but now there were no groceries to be seen. The cart was laden with junk—or so it appeared. An old coat lay next to a pile of newspapers, a pair of shoes rested against a camping stove. There were books and scarves, tins and cups, and she wouldn't leave it for a moment. Even when she fumbled in the dumpster, one hand stayed on the cart as if to protect the baggage of a life.

Look closer at her. It is you and I. We, like the bag-lady, push our yesterdays with us—the cart in which we have gathered memories, emotions, joys, and scars. And we push our carts straight into our relationships. We foolishly think that when we begin in marriage we come empty-handed but in reality we come clutching our past. And that past will often decide how we react to situations. Many of them will be trivial—the way we feel a meal should be prepared—but others will be deep; sometimes the baggage will affect our ability to give or receive love. And sometimes it will seem that even when we try to lay it down, the past will not die.

When I was a small boy there were very few "canned" frights to be had. We had no television and comics were tame. In fact we had only one bloodcurdling opportunity and it lay at the top of a small hill near my home. The title that we gave it seems now to lack a certain dramatic imagination, but in those far-off days it sent shivers down our spines. We called it, "The Haunted House." It was made of red brick, stood on about five acres of land, and had been empty for as long as anybody could remember. Rumor had it that the old boy, who had been dead at least twenty years, appeared now and again and Martin Davies from class 4B swore he had seen him. I spent long hours in that house peering behind bannisters and jumping every time a cat knocked over a tin in one of the outhouses, but I never did see the ghost.

But I have seen plenty since. Oh, not the kind that are apparitions, no these are too solid for that. One such time is still clear in my mind. It happened late on a Sunday evening in the heart of winter. Dianne and I were having a meal with a couple who had just returned from their honeymoon. He had cleaned the place up and she had cooked a wonderful meal. I have no doubt that they were out to impress us a little but that didn't bother us; soon they'd be like the rest of us just before visitors arrive—stuffing socks and empty potato chip bags under the cushions and trying to defrost a chicken in five minutes flat.

It was a perfect evening, that is until the dessert came. I'm no cook, but even I could tell that this sponge cake had an endearing Frisbee-like look. And that wouldn't have mattered a scrap if he hadn't made his little joke about it. Now I admit that I thought it looked like a Frisbee, but what I didn't know was that she was about to test its aerodynamics. It hit him square on. She burst into tears and ran out.

Dianne followed her upstairs and I helped him clear the cream off the curtains. He said to me, "What happened?"

I said, "A ghost visited us."

I could hear things quieting down upstairs but even so I guessed we had a little time and I began to tell him what I thought had happened. We began to talk about his father-in-law, a man I knew well. I believe that man had loved his wife, but for some reason best known to himself, he had constantly brought her down in public. I had heard her humiliated over her clothes, her weight, and yes, her cooking. The young woman now crying upstairs had watched her father break every ounce of self-esteem his wife might have had, and finally he had killed her love for him. When her mother had walked out three years before it wasn't in search of sex but of value.

I said, "Your new wife saw him in you. He is still alive–but it's as if a ghost came." He said very little, but something changed in him that night. It all happened many years ago and he has since became one of the most supportive husbands I have ever known.

The past can turn up at any moment and it is very strong, but we must acknowledge it and deal with it. It may mean stopping long enough to ask, "Why am I feeling this way?"; "Why am I saying these things?"; "Why is this such a big deal to me?" None of this is easy; it requires patience and understanding, but we *can* gain insights into the ways we react to certain situations. And it's not enough to see this ourselves; we need to be honest with our partner about our past hurts, heartbreaks, and disappointments. He or she deserves to know.

We can learn to recognize the old characteristics, the painful memories, the petty opinions–the things from yesterdays long gone that conspire to rob us of love today. And if we acknowledge it, so much of our behavior and reactions can be understood, and, just as importantly, changed.

It will help when ghosts come visiting.

ACTION PAGE

~ Lose some arguments.

~ Give your wife flowers when it's not her birthday or your anniversary.

~ Have a television-free evening occasionally.

~ When you get home, try to speak to your partner before doing anything else.

"The first duty of love is to listen."

– Paul Tillich

To Stay Sane as a Parent

I have some sympathy for the person who said, "Insanity is hereditary—you get it from your kids!" I don't think I could love my children more, but why didn't anybody warn us of the change they were going to cause in our relationship? One minute Dianne and I were spending our evenings taking walks together, visiting friends, and reading in front of the fire. The next we were walking the streets at midnight singing nursery rhymes and dealing with postpartum depression. (In me!)

And why didn't anybody get us ready for parenthood? For those of you who don't yet have children, Colin Bowles has devised twelve simple tests to see if you're ready. Here are three of them; if you fail these, skip the chapter on sex.

> Women: to prepare for maternity, put on a dressing gown and stick a beanbag down the front. Leave it there for nine months. After nine months take out 10% of the beans. Men: to prepare for paternity, go to the local pharmacy, tip the contents of your wallet on the counter, and tell the pharmacist to help himself. Then go to the supermarket. Arrange to

have your salary paid directly to their head office. Go home. Pick up the paper. Read it for the last time.

Can you stand the mess that children make? To find out, first smear peanut butter on the sofa and jelly on the curtains. Hide a fish stick behind the stereo and leave it there all summer. Stick your fingers in the flowerbeds then rub them on the clean walls. Cover the stains with crayon. How does that look?

Hollow out a melon. Make a small hole in the side. Suspend it from the ceiling and swing it from side to side. Now get a bowl of soggy cereal and attempt to spoon it into the swaying melon by pretending to be an airplane. Continue until half the cereal is gone. Tip the rest into your lap, making sure that a lot of it falls on the floor. You are now ready to feed a twelve-month-old baby.[4]

But those are the easy parts. Much harder is ensuring that while the relationship with this new person grows, the one with our partner doesn't die. I spend a fair amount of my time urging parents to spend time with their children; nevertheless when one parent becomes obsessed with a child to the exclusion of his or her partner, the marriage begins to operate as though there's an affair going on. And there is.

Here are ten keys to avoid your new baby driving you apart:

1. "The greatest thing parents can do for their children is to love each other." Dr. Benjamin Salk, family psychologist.

2. While giving your baby as much love as you can, be careful about protecting your own privacy. At times you'll want to let your baby share your bed but be wise as to how often. If space allows you may decide to let her sleep in a separate room as soon as possible.

3. Develop conversation that is not dominated by the latest in baby foods and teething rings.

4. Realize how easy it is for the father to feel both unneeded and excluded.

5. Share as many tasks as possible, even if this means they are not done to perfection. The baby will survive with a diaper half around his head.

6. Recognize how physically shattered many women are with the sheer effort of looking after a small baby.

7. If sex is not top of the agenda for a while, make sure this is not confused with rejection, and try to show intimacy in other ways.

8. Don't lose touch with your friends.

9. Don't refuse to let anybody else look after your child for a few hours. Some parents wouldn't allow Mary Poppins to baby-sit.

10. As the child grows, keep a sense of moderation in terms of your child's involvement in extra activities. You can exhaust yourselves and them quite easily. Ask yourself how important it is that a six-year-old can do ballet, kung-fu, and play three musical instruments.

Of course the truly sobering thing is that when this little baby hits thirteen, we will look back on those early years as though it was a permanent vacation. The problem with teenagers is that they sneak up on you. Whatever happened to that little girl who used to love holding your hand when you went shopping? Now she won't go out with you unless you've got a bag over your head. Where did that little boy disappear to who used to pour out the contents of his day to you as soon as he got home from school? Now, if you're lucky, you get a grunt.

Don't be disheartened if you're going through a tough time with your teenagers. It's hard for them as well. They are in that twilight world, balanced precariously between childhood and adulthood, and they're in the process of flexing their muscles a little. Hang in there; fight as few battles as possible; and don't worry about the grunting; when they hit twenty most of them start talking again.

But especially do not let these common hassles with teens drive you and your partner apart. It's not unusual for a child at this stage of life to give one of the parents a tougher time than the other, or even to play one off against the other. Stay together in it; talk issues through; try not to blame each other; and share your successes and failures with other parents—in other words, laugh at yourselves a little.

But above all give each other dignity in the task of parenthood. This is especially necessary for the parent who is at home looking after small children. So often society treats that person as if he or she has no proper job, and when a partner reaffirms that with comments like, "Well what have you been doing all day?" it really hits home. I have acted as a consultant to hundreds of businesses, most of them law firms. These are pretty complicated outfits with multi-task demands every minute. But I have never seen a task that comes close to the skills required to be a parent of small children.

Do You Work?

When you're at home with children the question you dread being asked at parties is, "Do you work?" I have some sympathy with the mother of three who replied like this:

> Actually I do work. I'm involved in a program of social development. At present I'm working with three age groups. First, toddlers: that involves a basic grasp of child psychology and

medicine. Second, teenagers," she said, "I confess the program is not going too well in that area. Thirdly, evenings and weekends I work with a man, aged thirty-nine, who is exhibiting all the classic symptoms of mid-life crisis—that's mainly psychiatric work. For the whole job you have to be a brilliant planner, have a "can-do" mentality and have a degree in conflict resolution. I used to be an international fashion model, but I got bored."

Support each other in the task of parenting, and keep a balance between commitment to them and to each other. It's important to make time for them but *it's even more vital to make time for each other.* They need you to keep your love alive.

Finally, from the day they are born get ready for the day when they will leave. It can happen so fast it will take your breath away. Give them all that you can, but don't build your lives solely around them. If you don't prepare for that day, in eighteen years you will get home from an airport somewhere, put the kettle on, look across at your partner and say, "Who are you?"

SIXTY-SECOND PAGE

"We can learn to recognize the old characteristics, the painful memories, the petty opinions–the things from yesterdays long gone that conspire to rob us of love today."

"When her mother had walked out three years ago it wasn't in search of sex but in search of value."

"When one parent becomes obsessed with a child to the exclusion of his or her partner the marriage begins to operate as though there's an affair going on. And there is."

"Don't be disheartened if you're going through a tough time with your teenagers. Hang in there. Fight as few battles as possible. When they hit twenty most of them start talking again."

"It's important to make time for your children but it's even more important to make time for each other. They need you to keep your love alive."

To Believe In Love Making

The couple sit quietly in the counseling room. We have talked about conflict, about communication, and then one of them will say, "And our sex life died years ago. It's not that we don't try but when I feel like it he doesn't, and then sometimes he's climbing the walls and all I want to do is sleep. I don't think anybody can help us now; it's gone too far."

Can this couple rediscover a sex life that's just a memory? Perhaps. But not unless they first dispel five myths that hit couple after couple.

Myth #1: "This is just us"

She made her way along the shelves of the bookstore. In front of her was an array of magazines and she glanced through the covers to find something that might interest her. Then she noticed it: "Great sex in your sixties!" She picked it up, scanned the article, and whispered under her breath, "I must be abnormal. I'm thirty-five, I've got a husband I love, and yet if one of the political parties promised to abolish sex tomorrow I'd vote for them. Why can't I feel like these sixty-year-olds who are leaping from the tops of wardrobes clothed in only a bus pass?"

One of the greatest difficulties to finding answers to problems in our sexual relationships in marriage is the belief that nobody else in the world could be experiencing what we're going through. And yet the opposite is true. Most marriages go through times when one of the partners is not interested in sex. Those could be times when desire seems to be at an all-time low, or just that at the end of the day he or she is too tired to think about sex, let alone do it. These are common situations, but just like other traumas that hit us in marriage we so often feel we're alone. But you're not; *this is not just you.*

This sense of isolation can be crushing at any time but especially when the whole world seems to be enjoying great sex all the time; that is if you believe some of the media which proclaim . . .

Myth #2:
Sex is always "absolutely fabulous"

Sarah and Neil had been married for just over six years and had a daughter, Samantha, aged three. Their only child was having her bedroom redecorated which meant that she had to be moved into her favorite sleeping venue in the whole world. Since early evening Samantha had been tucked up on a mattress at the foot of her parents' bed.

It was a Thursday, and for as long as they could remember Sarah and Neil had kept Thursday evenings for themselves. The "once a week date" idea was something an older couple had suggested to them just before they were married and they counted it high among the reasons they still had a strong relationship. By the time they got Samantha to bed and finally unplugged the phone it was eight o'clock. They had lit candles, devoured a pizza big enough to feed a football team, and watched *Sleepless in Seattle* on video (for the third time!). Just after midnight they entered a pitch black bedroom and, not wishing to wake their daughter, slid quietly into bed.

It was then that Neil decided to move across the bed towards his wife and in so doing initiated a conversation in stage whispers that could probably have been heard next door.

Sarah said, "Don't even think about it."

"But darling, she's fast asleep and we've had such a great evening."

"No!"

"Sarah don't do this to me."

"Neil, I don't think I'm Meg Ryan, and you are definitely not Tom Hanks, this is not the Empire State building and our daughter is asleep at the end of the bed–NO!"

"Darling . . . please."

At that moment another voice joined the conversation. It seemed to come from the foot of the bed and said, "Daddy! When Mommy says, 'No' she means 'No!'"

That kind of situation is not often found in the films; Hollywood sex is instant, perfect, and without a hint of disaster; real life can be a little harsher.

A honeymoon to remember

Tony and Claire are good friends of mine. Of course those aren't their real names, but with that slight change the rest of the story unfolds exactly as it happened:

> When they finally got to the hotel it was eleven o'clock at night. The room looked smaller than it had appeared in the brochure and Tony felt his heart sink. Just about the only contribution he had made to their wedding had been the choice of The Esplanade Hotel. It had been a long day, but apart from the agony of listening to almost ninety congratulatory cards being read aloud, and the best man making Claire's mother cry, the wedding had gone pretty well. But this was their honeymoon night. He desperately wanted this to be a memorable occasion.
>
> His spirits rose a little as they entered the room and he saw a ray of moonlight beaming through the window. This was going to be just perfect.
>
> And it may have been, had not the ray of moonlight illuminated two single beds. Tony rushed for the telephone and asked for the manager. "This is our honeymoon, and this is meant to be your honeymoon suite!" The manager was apologetic; there had been a double booking and the couple who had arrived at eight were well ensconced in the deluxe room with the four poster bed and jacuzzi.

"But there are single beds in here."

Then the manager suggested a solution which made Tony think that it was not the first time that The Esplanade had dealt with this particular problem. "I'll send up some rope and you can tie the beds together."

"Send it up fast!" said Tony.

So on the night that Tony had dreamed of for so many years, with the moon beams still flooding through the window and in the middle of his very best efforts, the beds parted. They crashed to the floor. Tony gazed up at a cracked ceiling and wanted to die right there and then, but Claire whispered to him, "Darling . . . I think I felt the earth move."

A bachelor asked a
computer to find him
the perfect partner:
"I want a companion who
is small and attractive,
loves water sports, and
enjoys group activities."

The computer answered,
"Marry a penguin."

If we are to have a good sexual relationship, one of the prerequisites is that we stop taking ourselves so seriously and quit imagining that our sex lives are going to impress Hollywood. In that particular suburb of Los Angeles, it seems that the sex is always wonderful. The beds are always made; the women look fantastic and seem to have an insatiable appetite for lovemaking. The men are animal-like and yet tender, rough yet smooth, and never fall asleep right afterwards. The real world is a little different. In the real world there are periods, mind-numbing tiredness, and children that are pre-timed to wake at the very hint of passion. Enjoy the films but don't compare your lovelife to them.

I get letters citing magazine articles stating that most couples enjoy sex 2.7 times a week. (Whatever is the .7?) The writers ask, "We don't have sex anything like that often; are we abnormal?" My reply is always the same: "Forget the statistics. It doesn't matter much whether you have sex 2.7 times a day, a week, or a month. What matters is that you both find a sexual expression that suits you."

Sex is an important part of marriage but it's not a measure of love. That statement is hard to believe in a Hollywood age, but it takes more than sex to build a relationship that can last.

Myth #3:
Great sex is always spontaneous

Come with me into a bedroom. It's eleven-thirty at night and the couple are about to have the argument of their life. But before we observe this drama let me take you back in time:

It's 3:00 P.M. Carla is on her way home from work. It had been as bad a day as she could remember but later she would look back on it as a haven of peace. On the way home she picks up Mark, aged two-and-a-half, from the baby-sitter and then rushes to the day care center to meet Simon, who is just six. Then, using skills she had picked up watching the Indianapolis 500, she pushes her car to the limit and gets to the elementary school just as Tom, her eight-year-old, is beginning to believe he had been abandoned by his mother–again!

She has just gotten all three of them into the back seat of the car when Mark begins to be sick. Any casual observer might have believed that had he wished to, he could have chosen to do so in any number of places. The fact that he picked the inside of Tom's new backpack displayed a degree of venom found only in the very young. The backseat erupts. Carla turns back to sort out the battle and narrowly misses knocking Tom's math teacher off his bicycle.

Halfway to the grocery store, Carla remembers Simon's dental appointment. The car performs the U-turn of its life as she heads for the other end of town. She is almost at the dentist's when she recalls Tom's piano class. The dilemma of having a child who can't play "Moonlight Sonata" or one with no teeth battles in her mind. She chooses to annoy the music teacher . . . again.

Eventually, complete with groceries, kids, and squelchy backpack, she staggers through the door. She begins dinner surrounded by a dog, a hamster on the loose, and a child complaining that the dentist took the wrong tooth out. She whispers under her breath, "If ever I leave home it will surely be at a quarter past five!"

The rest of the evening is a mixture of stories, glasses of water, and even more vomit. When this woman hits 11:00 P.M. she is practically comatose. When her husband suggests sex at 11:30 she refuses, and then as he lies with his back to her in his "hurt forever" position, she begins to feel guilty. She wonders "Am I abnormal?"

The answer is "No—just sane."

I quite understand that the scenario could be reversed, although I must say that most men seem to be able to be at death's door and still feel like sex. In any event, times when we feel shattered are not the best to develop a good sex life.

For that very reason many couples have discovered that "planned sex" is not such a bad idea.

One husband put it like this:

> "I know it sounds a bit clinical but life is so hectic we found that if we didn't plan ahead we were just too tired for sex. I'm not saying it will work for everybody, but we have come to regard those nights as special. Even then we don't always have sex, but we make room both in time

and emotionally. Of course it can still happen spontaneously, but we're beginning to see the value of taking our sexual relationship seriously."

"Couples say they don't have time for sex, but so often it's because they don't make time."

–Jim Boston,
Psycho-sexual therapist

Myth #4:
Relationship doesn't matter

There are plenty of marriages where it is the wife who wants sex more than the husband; nevertheless it's very common for us to hear from husbands, "My wife's not interested in sex." When we are counseling we will often ask a couple, "If you could change anything in your relationship, what would it be?" The man will usually answer "Sex. I wish my wife wanted sex more often." We turn to the woman. She pauses and then says, "Affection. I wish he was more affectionate." We ask, "How could he show that to you?" She will say, "I would love him to sometimes touch me in a non-sexual way–just out of affection. I wish that some nights he would just hold me when we are in bed together. I wish when we shop together he would occasionally hold my hand instead of walking ten yards ahead. I want him to listen to me when I share my heart. I want to know I matter."

The comment this woman made about touch is a powerful one. Some years ago Dianne and I met a woman of seventy-five who had started to learn ballroom dancing. Dianne said, "You must enjoy it." She replied, "Oh, I do, my dear. But the real reason I go is that it's the only time in the week when anybody touches me."

Myth #5: *"Our sex life is gone forever"*

I know it's not true. I meet many couples who rediscover a sexual relationship with their partner that they believed could never return. After almost fifteen years of marriage Kevin decided to do something about their sex life other than complain. He began to go out with his wife alone rather than always with friends; he stopped complaining about the few extra pounds she had put on and started to compliment her again; he began to touch her more; and most important of all, he did all of that without any expectation of sex later that day. Their sex life changed when his wife began to believe that she mattered.

We can find answers. A sixty-year-old man came up to me after one of our seminars. He told me he and his wife had rediscovered a sex life that was better than ever before. Some are helped by seeing a professional counselor, others by reading a book, but countless more by being real, and remembering that the sex therapist was right who said, "If a man wants a wild Friday night he had better start working on it Monday morning!"

I suppose that shouldn't be surprising; after all—it is *love* making.

ACTION PAGE

~ Hold hands more often.

~ Practice touching in a nonsexual way.

~ Let your children see that you respect your partner.

~ Try not to be completely predictable.

Love is patient, love is kind.
It does not envy, it does not
boast, it is not proud. It is not
rude, it is not self-seeking, it is
not easily angered, it keeps
no record of wrongs. Love
does not delight in evil but
rejoices with the truth. It
always protects, always trusts,
always hopes, always
perseveres. Love never fails.

*— The New Testament,
1 Corinthians 13:4-8a*

To Deal with Debt

Helen still remembers it clearly; it was Christmas Eve and the supermarket was overflowing. On the same day last year she had vowed she would never leave it this late again but here she was fighting through the crowds, trying hard to steer the grocery cart so as not to take the heels off the man in front (again!) and all the time with a three-year-old clinging to her coat declaring, "No," she could not wait until they got home.

If somebody had told her the long lines had been for a night out with Richard Gere or Cindy Crawford she could have understood it, but it was hard to believe that grown men and women would stand in line all the way back down the aisles with a basket containing only chocolate and six oranges. But eventually she made it to the checkout and the "next customer please" sign emerged like an angel from the morass of food the man in front had piled on the counter.

She had just finished packing it all when it happened. The girl at the checkout said, "I'm sorry, your bank card has been rejected." The people in the line behind Helen were showing a mixture of annoyance and unhealthy interest. She fumbled in her bag for another credit card, but that too was over the limit. She grabbed her daughter, left the bags of food where they were and ran out of the store. On the day after New Year's she began divorce proceedings.

You may think her rash, but actually the Christmas Eve supermarket incident wasn't the first. Brian had been a good husband and father but he couldn't handle money. There had been dozens of bank manager's letters, a car repossessed, and every time an ATM paid out cash Helen felt a wave of relief.

It was hard to remember exactly when it had all gone wrong. When they were first married they had little money but seemed to get along pretty well. It is true that some of the furniture was second-hand and they didn't have such expensive holidays, but they always managed; they even saved a little. I suppose it changed on the day the letter came.

> Dear Mr. and Mrs. Kent,
> Have you ever wondered what it would be like to have $10,000 to spend exactly as you want? It could be a well-deserved vacation, a new car, or that kitchen you've always dreamed about.
> Well you do have the money! You have been specially selected and all you need to do is to call the toll-free phone number and your check could be with you in just three days. You can already feel the sun on that exotic vacation!

It seemed so easy and the repayment schedule convinced them they could afford it. They opted for the ten-year plan. The APR was 17.5%. They remember laughing because neither of them knew what APR stood for! The first thing they did was take that vacation; heaven knows they both needed it. And the next . . . well that's the hard part. They knew it sounded stupid but they just aren't sure where the rest went. They took out the loan on June 1. When they got back from Majorca on August 1, they had exactly nine years and ten months left to repay it. The total cost– $20,326.26.

Just as well they had the credit cards. When they had taken them out the advertising blurb had said if they paid them off at the end of each month they could have up to six weeks free credit! With the ten-year loan around their necks they were in need of something free. It's just that it never happened. They always paid the minimum. Soon they were paying interest on interest. But it didn't matter because everybody seemed to be offering them a credit card. And they were so convenient. They used them everywhere. They even went to the movies on credit.

At the end of that year they had acquired four credit cards and had a total debt on them of $16,000. They were sinking fast.

The rescue should have come the following February. Brian got promotion and a salary increase of $2,500 a year. The extra fifty dollars a week should have given them more than enough. But it didn't. Every month they were still overdrawn, and in May the bank refused to pay the standing order for the mortgage. Helen came to believe that no matter how large the raise, it still wouldn't have sorted them out. She was right.

Brian and Helen were now in a situation that affects millions of people, whatever their income; they had fallen into the 10 percent trap. It is simply that whatever our income, we spend approximately 10 percent more.

One of the most frightening things about debt is that it isolates us. It makes us feel there is nobody else in the world who could have gotten into such a mess. You may be in that situation right now. If so the first thing to know is that you're not alone. Others have been in this situation and come out of it. The average debt in this country is now over $5,000 per family in credit cards alone.[5] And debt puts tremendous pressures on family life. In fact a large percentage of marriages that break up say financial trouble was at the heart of the problem.

The second thing to realize is you can get out of the debt trap. I confess it won't be as easy as getting into it, but it can happen. Of course it depends how much you owe and how disciplined you are, but if you use the following ten principles you'll begin to see a difference after just one month.

Talk it over together

The hardest debt to talk about in a marriage is "private debt." By this I mean borrowing which your partner doesn't know about. Your husband may know you sometimes buy clothes from a catalog but he has no idea just how high that debt has risen. Your wife knows you've got that extra credit card "just for emergencies." What she doesn't know is you started using it six months ago and it's already up to the limit. Again, remember you're not alone. You're not the only one in the whole country rushing to get to the mailbox before your partner, but it's a draining business and it normally comes to light eventually. You may be the partner who has to receive the bad news; if so realize how hard it was for your partner to tell you and although you may feel both hurt and worried, try to see this as a first step to getting your finances under control.

Debt thrives when we just don't know where we are with our money. When we're in this situation we're never sure what figure will be at the bottom of the bank statement; we're always using the cash machine but never sure where the money goes; and couldn't really say how much we owe at any one time. The next three steps aim to put you back in control, because at the end of these you'll know your exact financial position.

Make a list of all your outstanding debts
Put down everything; at this stage it's better to know the worst.

Make a list of all your income
Use the figure after taxes and don't include things like bonuses unless they have become a regular part of

your income. Remember to check that you are receiving all the government benefits to which you are entitled. Call your local Consumer Credit Counseling Service for help on this.

Make a list of all expenditures

This is the hardest part, and the big temptation here is just to put the big items down, but include everything–newspapers, sodas, dry cleaning–EVERYTHING!

Many people find that their expenditure is always slightly higher than income. They cover this by overdrafts, or credit cards.

Prepare a budget

The aim now is to reduce expenditures so that they are lower than your income. Prepare another expenditure list, but this time made up of how you intend to spend your money in the future. Keep working on this until you get it below income. You won't be able to do much about mortgage or rent payments, but find things that can be reduced.

Stay in control

Once a month sit down together with your bank statements, credit card receipts, and any outstanding bills and assess how you are doing.

Repay

As soon as you can afford it, begin to pay more than the minimum off your credit card bills. The aim here is to reduce the amount of debt on which you are paying interest. Think carefully about each use of ATM machines. Decide on an amount of cash you will withdraw each week and try to stick to it.

Stay in touch

If you are worried because people to whom you owe money are threatening to take you to court, write to them and let them see your income and expenditure figures. Most of the people they pursue never reply, and you'll be able to show that although you may have made mistakes in the past, you are trying to sort it out now. Offer them what you can afford—even if it's only a few dollars a month.

Rediscover cash

Consider going back to cash for a while. When we use credit cards we spend about a third more; they whisper to us, "This is not real money." The first credit card advertisement said, "Take the waiting out of wanting." Put the waiting back in and pay them less interest. If you are in real difficulty on your credit cards it may be best to cut them in half and send them back to the credit card companies. Tell them of your difficulty; they will sometimes freeze interest while you try to repay your balance owed.

Keep a large trash can next to your stack of mail

The next time somebody offers you the lending deal of a lifetime use the trash can immediately. Develop the technique of "smelling out" credit offers and throw those away without opening the envelope.

And what about Helen, the woman who left her Christmas shopping on the checkout counter? She never did go through with that divorce. She persuaded Brian to walk into a debt counseling center and he fought for his marriage. It took them two years to get their finances under control. They now manage to save a little each month. Brian said to us recently, "The sense of being in control is fantastic." It's true that it wasn't without cost, but then again they weren't just fighting for the money.

And a three-year-old still has a father.

SIXTY-SECOND PAGE

"Brian and Helen were now in a situation that affects millions of people, whatever their income. They had fallen into the 10 percent trap. It is simply that *whatever* our income we spend approximately 10 percent more."

"Once a month sit down together with your bank statements, credit card receipts, and any outstanding bills; assess how you are doing."

"Consider going back to cash for a while. When we use credit cards we spend about a third more–they whisper to us. 'This is not real money.'"

"One of the greatest difficulties to finding answers to problems we may be experiencing in our sexual relationship is the belief that nobody else in the world could be experiencing what we're going through. But most marriages go though times when one of the partners is not interested in sex."

"Couples say they don't have time for sex but so often it's because they don't make time."

"Sex is an important part of marriage but don't see it as a measure of love."

To Think Twice—for the Sake of the Children

One of the most moving pieces of television I have ever seen was a "Panorama"[6] television program that examined the effect of family break-up on children. It was called, "For the Sake of the Children." Several couples who had split up were interviewed and the effects of their divorces on their children were examined. The overwhelming sense was that these men and women had done all they could to help their children through the trauma of the break-up of their family. But one small boy, named Stuart, could not be consoled.

Stuart was nine, and as the interviewer, and later a counselor, sought to ask him questions his eyes would fill up and he would begin to cry uncontrollably. Time and time again he expressed his wish that his parents be back together again. At times he would be holding onto both—determined not to show favoritism. His father had left some six years previously but it was evident that he loved his son; in fact as the boy cried the father did too. He was by now in a new relationship and so was the mother. They dealt with each other with dignity and it was apparent that they had done all they felt they could to make their break-up as painless as possible for their children.

Nevertheless, as they spoke it was evident that they were shocked by the severity of the reaction their parting had caused in Stuart's life.

One of the most vital parts of the work in which I have been involved in recent years has been supporting single parents; they have one of the most difficult tasks on the face of the earth. That has involved running vacations for single parents and their children, counseling, and answering the many letters that come from those in this situation. In that correspondence there are recurring themes—financial hardship, loneliness, and the sheer hard work of bringing up a child alone. But deeper than all of these is often a concern at how the children are coping with the loss of a parent (usually a father).

Facing the Issue

As a society we have often hidden from people the effect of family break-up on children. We may do this out of kindness, feeling that divorce is hard enough without putting people on a guilt trip over the children. Or it may be that we do not tackle this issue because of ignorance. For the past thirty years we have often heard it said, "Divorce for the sake of the children." It has been claimed that children are better when removed from a home with conflict and they will be happier when the parents split. Subsequent studies are causing us to realize the devastating effect that divorce itself can have on children, lasting in some cases into adulthood.

We are used to blaming the media for all manner of things but I believe that in recent years the media has performed a vital function in highlighting the real effect of family break-up on children.

This is how one newspaper put it:

> "What happens to your children if you or your partner dies? You have probably taken out life insurance with such a possibility in mind. . . . But have you thought about what may happen if you divorce or separate? You probably haven't thought as much about it as you have the possibility of dying. . . . This is a pity because children are damaged much more by divorce than they are by their parent's death."[7]

The above piece was part of an article reporting on the research of Dr. Martin Richards; he runs the Center for Family Research at Cambridge University. He explains why family break-up is so devastating for children: "Low self-esteem may underlie a lot of these effects. The death of a parent doesn't produce the same problems. The critical thing seems to be children's awareness that parents have through choice decided to separate, and for many this means a parent choosing to leave them."[8] He goes on to catalog the physical and emotional effects that can occur. He is not a lone voice. This is what other researchers have said:

It is well established that children whose parents divorce commonly go through a crisis period at the time of separation from which they recover with varying degrees of resilience and speed. For some there may be long-term consequences. . . . The chances have been shown to be greater, for example, of leaving school at the minimum age, failing to obtain educational qualifications, leaving home due to friction, cohabitation, marriage and childbearing at an early age and of poor mental health.[9]

–David Utting,
The Joseph Rowntree Foundation

Children whose families have been "re-ordered" by separation and divorce were more likely than children from intact families to have encountered health problems (especially psychosomatic disorders), to have needed extra help at school, to have experienced friendship difficulties and to suffer from low self-esteem.[10]

– Dr. John Tripp and Monica Cockett,
Department of Child Health, Postgraduate
Medical School, Exeter University

Studies in Britain and the United States strongly suggest that divorce has an impact on children that lasts into adulthood and affects their personal relationships later on.[11]

– Anthony Clare,
Professor of Clinical Psychology

I see too much pain on a daily basis to believe that these are easy issues. When we are in the middle of trauma in our relationships, when all we want to do is to be gone and start a new life, it's hard to consider logically what is best for the children. The easiest thing to think is, "If I'm happy then they'll be happy." But so often that is wrong. And afterwards it's hard to understand why they should be so badly affected because now there's no arguing and no shouting, and they don't see Mom crying all the time or Dad sitting with his head in his hands. Life in so many ways is easier. But they are devastated.

I suppose this shouldn't be all that surprising; although the partners may feel they have stopped loving each other, the children still love both parents; and they want both of them. The vast majority of parents try with all their hearts to minimize the effects of family break-up on children but you cannot lose somebody you love, somebody you thought was going to be around for you until you were grown, without knowing incredible trauma.

One More Look

May I say a brief word to a father who may be considering leaving his family? You believe your marriage is over and in fact you have been seeing someone else for a while now. Soon you will tell your wife and this will begin a process that will lead to your leaving your home and your children. Were we to meet, you would tell me of the agony of the past few years and how tough it's been, and that you feel you've done all you can. Well, perhaps you have, but do this one more thing. Tonight go to your children's bedrooms when they are asleep and stand there for a while. Allow your mind to go back over the years you have had with them, and then try to imagine how they are going to need you in the future.

I don't know whether that simple act will change your mind about leaving, although with all my heart I hope it will; but I can tell you something with certainty: many people will write to me and tell me that asking you to spend those couple of minutes in that room was a waste of time—that it was naïve and too emotional.

But you won't be one of them.

THE ONE-SECOND PAGE

It may not always be
right to stay together
"for the sake
of the children."

But it's still a good reason.

ACTION PAGE

~ Eat a meal by candlelight occasionally.

~ Develop a pastime that you both enjoy.

~ Before starting an argument ask, "Is this worth fighting over?"

~ Keep your promises.

GOAL TEN

To Dispel the Illusions

I sit at the back of the church and watch the young couple. The bridegroom is the son of a close friend. He looks handsome, she incredibly beautiful. I allow my eyes to scan the church. There are hats of all shapes, men tugging at the collars of over-tight shirts, and a small ring bearer trying to pull the hair of a bridesmaid in front of him. The fragrance of fresh cut flowers fills the building and sun streams through the stained glass. It is in every sense a perfect day, and not even the thought of standing in a long receiving line can dampen the sense of completeness I feel at this moment.

Yet I spend my life dealing with relationships that have broken; love that began as this one does today, filled with hope and optimism. And I wonder as I sit and watch that if somebody said, "You have just ten minutes to pass on some counsel to this couple as they begin their life together," what I would say to them.

I decide that I would ask them to consider something that on this day seems impossible; to imagine that the day may come when they feel their love is at an end and it's time to leave each other. I will tell them of the three great illusions that they will have to overcome if their love is to survive through that arid period.

Illusion #1:
Nothing could ever change for us now

Sometimes people say to me, "But some marriages are surely over." Well, perhaps they are, but don't ask me to tell you which ones. Over the years I have seen countless couples whose marriages seemed to be dead decide to fight to keep their family together, and some in this process have found a love they thought was gone forever.

Some of those have been situations where for years one of the partners has been trying to change the other. And then one day they decided to change themselves in some way. They used to have a tongue that sprang quickly to criticism but they began to praise; they used to be closed emotionally but they began to share; they used to always be in control of everything but they began to show vulnerability and a need of their partner. And then they discovered something by surprise: that because change is dynamic it's almost impossible that it does not affect the other person. See for example this letter I received:

> You may not remember me but we talked with you about problems in our marriage. It is only fair to let you know how things have developed since. The change that has occurred is,

humanly speaking, impossible. This is not just a feeling—even the children have commented on it. They have known that Peter loves them, but they have not known how to relate to him. But their love for their Dad has grown and is visible. This is the marriage I dreamed of twenty years ago! I have wanted to tell you earlier but somehow now it seems more real because it has stood the test of time.

Illusion #2:
Life would be so different with another person

This illusion is not so easy to spot because of course in some ways it is true. Life would be different. But would it be better? We say, "Anything would be better than this." Perhaps.

The affair is a good example of this illusion. Very few people go looking for an affair. But it often happens when we feel that the person we are with isn't all we want them to be and then we meet somebody who promises to fulfill our dreams. Our husband is inattentive but *he* listens carefully; our wife has become dull but *she* is vibrant. For the first time in years we feel truly alive. This is the person we should have married.

It was December and the office was having its annual Christmas lunch-hour drink. When David entered the restaurant the noise hit him like a wall, and for a while he had trouble focusing, but then he saw somebody from the marketing department at a table in the window. She'd only just joined the firm and he didn't even know her name. They had both arrived early and in no time at all had started chatting.

He can remember thinking as he walked back to the office how much easier she was to talk to than Sarah.

They saw each other quite a lot after that. If you'd have told him when he walked the ten yards across the floor of that restaurant towards the window table that they would have gotten so close he wouldn't have believed you. They hadn't planned anything; it had "just happened." She was having a tough time in her marriage and said he was so understanding.

They began sleeping together in March.

He loved Sarah, or he thought he did, but Carol made him feel half of his forty-two years. He found himself thinking about her all the time, imagining the meetings, almost enjoying the thrill of keeping it a secret from the rest of the office.

In June she moved out of her home and into an apartment. She told him that he hadn't broken up her marriage; it would have happened anyway; it was over. And suddenly he had to decide. He felt like a child. The truth was he wanted both. He wanted Sarah and the children and he wanted her. On September 1 he decided. It was better for everybody.

And now he stands in the hall of his home, suitcases in hand. His daughter stands with his wife and they watch him in unbelief as if a play is unfolding. He says, "I never meant to hurt you all." We wonder what is ahead for him. I can't be sure, but I can tell you what is common.

The grass is always greener

He and the new woman in his life will build a lovenest. Into this haven will come no crying children; there will be no endless demands to help with chores, or bodies to be ushered to piano class. The sex will be incredible, and the conversation captivating, and when he wakes and sees her sleeping there he will wonder if he ever did love Sarah.

This may last for two years. Then without warning, a principle will come into force that will rock him to his heels. It was coined by Dr. James Dobson: "The other man's grass may be greener—but it still needs mowing."

And the ordinary will invade their lives. Who would have thought that the tap would have leaked here in this new life as it always did in the bathroom at home and who could have predicted an evening when one of them would say, "No, not tonight. And did you put the trash out?"

Who could have told him that he would begin to dream that he is back in the restaurant and he is walking the ten yards again, but this time they lead him to a different table. And in these dreams he will be telling his children a story and bandaging a cut knee.

But he knows little of that now as he stands in the hallway with his brand new suitcases on his way to his brand new relationship, in his search for the person who will fulfill his dreams.

I have heard his story countless times. I remember speaking to a man who had just left his wife. He said, "The sex with my wife wasn't very good, but the sex with this woman is fantastic." I said to him, "There's never been an affair in the history of the world where the sex hasn't been fantastic." Then I said, "But you have a child just six months old. He didn't ask you to bring him into the world. You talk of your rights, but what about his? He has rights to stories from you, and guidance from you, and protection from you. You are his father."

It's hard to think of that when the illusion first hits. But perhaps George Bernard Shaw was right:

> "There are two great tragedies in life: one is not to get the desire of your heart. The other is to get it."

Illusion #3:
Real love is just a feeling

It is impossible for love to be sustained by feelings alone. Every marriage goes through a time where at least one of the partners does not feel in love. At such a time everything screams out, "Let go, it's over." But if we do let go the first time that happens, we will never find a love that lasts.

We live in a society in which we are told we deserve the best. Can that be true in marriage? Are we to love so long as we have the best–someone attractive, witty, who goes on meeting all our needs? No–if we are to find real love we will have to learn to love against the odds.

In his book *Mortal Lessons: Notes in the Art of Surgery,* Richard Seltzer, a surgeon, recounts the following incident:

> I stand by the bed where a young woman lies, her face postoperative, her mouth twisted in palsy, clownish. A tiny twig of the facial nerve, the one to the muscles of her mouth has been severed. She will be thus from now on. The surgeon has followed with religious fervor the curve of her flesh, I promise you that. Nevertheless to remove the tumor in her cheek I have cut a little nerve. Her young husband is in the room. He stands on the opposite side of the bed and together they seem to dwell in the evening lamp light, isolated from me, private. "Who are they?" I ask myself, "He and this wry mouth that I have made. Who gaze at and touch each other so greedily." The young woman speaks. "Will my mouth always be like this?" she asks. "Yes it will," I say. "It is because

the nerve was cut." She nods and is silent, but the young man smiles. "I like it," he says, "It's kind of cute." And all at once I know who he is and I lower my gaze. . . . And unmindful I see he bends to kiss her crooked mouth, and I so close, I can see how he twists his own lips to accommodate hers, to show the kiss still works. . . . And I hold my breath, and let the wonder in.[12]

Would that young husband have preferred his wife to have had the looks she had when he married her? Of course. Is it the case that sometimes even now he dreams of her with a perfect face? Yes. But there will come to every marriage a time when we are called to love not "because of" but "in spite of," a time when we have to twist our lips "to show the kiss still works." It has at its heart not just the feeling of love but the *will* to love. Unless we hold on during that time it is impossible for love to last.

ACTION PAGE

~ Take a trip down memory lane: have an
evening with your old photographs.

~ Revisit some of the places that were favorites
when you first met.

~ Try to laugh more together.

~ When your partner says "I love you," don't
discuss it–just accept it.

SIXTY-SECOND PAGE

"Parents try with all their hearts to minimize the effects of family break-up on children but you cannot lose somebody you love, somebody you thought was going to be around for you until you were grown up, without knowing incredible trauma."

"Over the years I have seen countless couples whose marriage seemed to be dead, decide to fight to keep their family together and some in that very process have found a love they thought was gone forever."

"There will come a time in every marriage when we are called to love not 'because of' but 'in spite of.' It has at its heart not just the feeling of love but the *will* to love. Unless we hold on to that, it is impossible for love to last."

Epilogue

Our sixty minutes is almost over. We have considered many things together—conflict and money, sex and ghosts to name just a few. But is there a theme running through it all? Come back for a moment to that wedding. As I sit and listen they begin their vows and I realize that these lines, now hundreds of years old, contain a key to marriage that in modern society we have all but lost. In short they dare to invade this perfect day with warnings of darker times ahead. She says "I will love you if you are well . . . and if you are sick." He replies, "If we are rich . . . and if we are poor." The vows whisper to them, "Enjoy your happiness, but if love is to last you must learn to love in harder times." Will those vows ever be called in? As sure as night follows day they will be; and at that moment the feeling of love alone will not sustain this couple. They may have a lifetime together when they will become not just lovers but friends, but there will be times during which they will have to fight to keep love alive.

Some of those times will be short and quickly forgotten; others will be prolonged and very difficult. And by then it may not be just the two of them who are affected, and small children also will be watching this drama of relationship being acted out.

So come with me one last time, back to the start of *The Sixty-Minute Marriage Builder* and the scene with which we began. Emily is still there, foot swinging over the edge of the seat, still throwing peanuts to the sparrows. She represents the children who have no say in their parents' affairs, who in that sense are too young to have a voice. In *The Sixty-Minute Marriage Builder* I wanted to say something to help the young couple in their new relationship, to strengthen the hands of those who have good marriages, and to hold out some hope to those going though traumatic times. Almost all we have considered together is relevant whether or not we have children of our own, but I confess that so often as I wrote, it was the child at the zoo that filled my sight. I thought of her rights, and her needs, and her future, and I wanted to speak for her.

It was for Emily's sake.

Notes

1. NOP Consumer Market Research on fathering carried out for CARE for the Family, January 1995. Available from CARE for the Family, Cardiff, Wales.

2. Dr. James Dobson, *Straight Talk to Men and Their Wives* (Word, Inc.: Dallas Texas, 1980). All rights reserved.

3. Marc Cohn, "The Things We've Handed Down," from the album *The Rainy Season*, Atlantic Records, 1993 (London: Gelfand, Rennert, and Felman). Used with permission.

4. Colin Bowles, *The Beginners Guide to Fatherhood* (HarperCollins Publishers Limited: London, 1992).

5. Keith Tondeur, "Escape from Debt," published by Credit Action, 1993.

6. "Panorama," BBC Television, 7 February 1994.

7. Ian Robertson, "How Children are Affected by Divorce," *The Times* (London), 2 May 1995.

8. Ibid.

9. David Utting, *Family and Parenthood: Supporting Families, Preventing Breakdown. A Guide to the Debate*, Joseph Rowntree Foundation, February 1995.

10. *Findings Bulletin*, No. 45, February 1994, Joseph Rowntree Foundation.

11. "Why Parents Should Not Be Allowed to Divorce," *Daily Mail* (London), 28 April 1994.

12. Richard Seltzer, *Mortal Lessons: Notes in the Art of Surgery*, by permission of the author c/o Rogers, Coleridge & White Ltd., 20 Powis Mews, London W11 1JN in association with George Borchardt Inc., 136 East 57th Street, New York, NY 10011.